Master Generative AI in Minutes

Advanced Strategies, Practical Solutions, and Case Studies for Busy Professionals

CONSULTORIA IA

Master Generative AI in Minutes

Advanced Strategies, Practical Solutions, and Case Studies for Busy Professionals

CONSULTORIA IA

Consultoria IA

Master Generative AI in Minutes

Advanced Strategies, Practical Solutions, and Case Studies for Busy Professionals

Copyright © 2024 by Consultoria IA

All rights reserved. No part of this publication may be reproduced, stored or transmitted in any form or by any means, electronic, mechanical, photocopying, recording, scanning, or otherwise without written permission from the publisher. It is illegal to copy this book, post it to a website, or distribute it by any other means without permission.

First edition

This book was professionally typeset on Reedsy
Find out more at reedsy.com

Contents

Master Generative AI in Minutes: Advanced Strategies, Practical Solutions, and Case Studies for Busy Professionals

Brief overview

Target Audience

Why Read this book

Preface

Chapter 1: Unlocking the Power of Generative AI: Core Concepts in Record Time

Chapter 2: Rapid Implementation Strategies for Professionals

Chapter 3: Advanced Techniques: Beyond the Basics

Chapter 4: Practical Applications Across Industries

Chapter 5: Future-Proofing Your Skillset with Generative AI

Appendices for Master Generative AI in Minutes: Advanced Strategies, Practical Solutions, and Case Studies for Busy Professionals

Master Generative AI in Minutes: Advanced Strategies, Practical Solutions, and Case Studies for Busy Professionals

Brief overview

M**aster Generative AI in Minutes: Advanced Strategies, Practical Solutions, and Case Studies for Busy Professionals** is a concise yet comprehensive guide tailored for professionals seeking to harness the power of generative AI in their industries. Packed with actionable strategies, real-world case studies, and practical solutions, this ebook simplifies complex concepts into digestible insights. Perfect for busy individuals, it offers tools to innovate workflows, enhance decision-making, and stay ahead in the fast-evolving digital landscape. Whether you're in business, tech, or creative fields, this resource equips you with the expertise to unlock AI's full potential in just minutes.

Target Audience

The target audience for the ebook *"Master Generative AI in Minutes: Advanced Strategies, Practical Solutions, and Case Studies for Busy Professionals"* would be:

Busy professionals looking to quickly understand and apply generative AI concepts to their work.

Executives and managers who need a practical overview of how generative AI can create value in their industries.

Entrepreneurs and startups interested in leveraging AI-driven solutions for innovation and competitive advantage.

Technology consultants and advisors aiming to expand their knowledge of AI to better serve their clients.

Industry leaders and decision-makers seeking actionable insights and case studies to inform strategic planning.

Educators and trainers in AI who require concise, practical content for teaching purposes.

This audience appreciates efficiency, actionable insights, and real-world applications.

Why Read this book

The ebook *"Master Generative AI in Minutes: Advanced Strategies, Practical Solutions, and Case Studies for Busy Professionals"* addresses the following problems:

Lack of Time to Learn AI Concepts

Provides concise, focused information tailored to busy schedules, enabling professionals to grasp complex generative AI concepts quickly.

Understanding Practical Applications

Bridges the gap between theory and practice by offering real-world examples and case studies that demonstrate how generative AI can solve specific business challenges.

Difficulty in Implementing AI Solutions

Offers actionable strategies and step-by-step guidance to help professionals implement generative AI solutions effectively.

Staying Competitive in the Market

Equips readers with the knowledge to leverage AI for innovation, efficiency, and maintaining a competitive edge.

Overcoming Technological Intimidation

Simplifies advanced AI concepts into digestible content, making it accessible to those without technical expertise.

Lack of Resources for Quick Adoption

Serves as a practical resource with strategies, tools, and frameworks to integrate generative AI into existing workflows.

Navigating Ethical and Operational Challenges

Provides insights into managing ethical considerations and addressing potential risks associated with generative AI use.

This book is a toolkit for professionals seeking to make informed decisions and implement AI-driven solutions in their fields.

Preface

In today's fast-paced world, innovation waits for no one. The rise of generative AI has transformed the way we approach creativity, problem-solving, and decision-making across industries. Yet, for busy professionals, diving deep into complex AI technologies often feels like a daunting, time-consuming task. That's where this book comes in.

Master Generative AI in Minutes: Advanced Strategies, Practical Solutions, and Case Studies for Busy Professionals is designed with you in mind—the busy executive, entrepreneur, or industry leader who needs results now. Whether you're a decision-maker looking to stay ahead of the curve, a consultant guiding clients through AI adoption, or an innovator building the next big thing, this book delivers what you need: actionable insights, real-world applications, and a clear roadmap for leveraging generative AI in your work.

This is not a textbook filled with jargon and theories; it's a practical guide to mastering the tools, strategies, and ethical considerations that matter in the real world. You'll find case studies that illustrate success stories, frameworks to navigate challenges, and step-by-step solutions for deploying generative AI effectively.

Generative AI is no longer a futuristic concept—it's here, reshaping industries from marketing to medicine, from design to data analysis. This book is your shortcut to understanding how to use it, without wading through endless research or sacrificing your productivity.

Let's unlock the power of generative AI together, one minute at a time.
CONSULTORIA IA

Chapter 1: Unlocking the Power of Generative AI: Core Concepts in Record Time

Generative AI is undoubtedly one of the most transformative technologies of our time. Its potential to revolutionize industries, enhance creativity, and streamline business processes is immense. This chapter aims to unlock the core concepts of generative AI in record time, providing busy professionals with a quick yet thorough understanding of the technology, its underlying principles, and its vast applications. Through a combination of theoretical insights, data-driven analysis, and expert citations, we will explore the essentials of generative AI, shedding light on its significance in today's world.

1.1 Defining Generative AI

Generative AI refers to a subset of artificial intelligence systems designed to generate new, original content—whether text, images, music, code, or other forms of data—based on patterns learned from existing data. Unlike traditional AI, which focuses on recognizing patterns and making predictions, generative AI is specifically trained to create new data that mimics real-world distributions. This ability to generate realistic and novel content makes generative AI a powerful tool in diverse fields, from content creation and entertainment to healthcare and engineering.

The term "generative" is crucial here. It distinguishes these systems from other forms of AI, such as discriminative models, which predict a specific output given an input (e.g., classifying an image). Generative models, by contrast, learn the underlying structure of the input data and use that understanding to produce new examples that resemble the original data. This process often involves sophisticated neural networks, particularly generative adversarial networks (GANs) and variational autoencoders (VAEs), both of which will be explored in more detail later.

1.2 Key Components of Generative AI

To understand how generative AI works, we must break down its key components:

Data Input: Like any AI model, generative AI requires data to learn from. This data can range from images, text, and audio to more complex data structures such as medical records or financial transactions. The quality and quantity of the input data are critical for the performance of generative models.

Model Architecture: At the heart of generative AI lies the model architecture. The most common architectures include:

Generative Adversarial Networks (GANs): Introduced by Ian Goodfellow in 2014, GANs consist of two neural networks: a generator and a discriminator. The generator creates fake data, while the discriminator evaluates it against real data. The two networks are locked in a competition, with the generator attempting to fool the discriminator. This adversarial setup allows GANs to produce highly realistic content.

Variational Autoencoders (VAEs): VAEs, developed by Kingma and Welling in 2013, focus on probabilistic modeling. They encode input data into a latent space and decode it to generate new samples. VAEs are often used in scenarios where the focus is on generating diverse outputs with smooth transitions.

Transformers: While originally designed for natural language processing (NLP), transformer models, such as OpenAI's GPT (Generative Pre-trained Transformer), have been widely adopted in generative AI tasks. These models use self-attention mechanisms to process sequences of data, enabling them to generate high-quality text, images, and even code.

Training Process: Generative AI models are trained using large datasets, employing various training techniques to minimize error and improve output quality. Training often requires significant computational resources, particularly for large models with billions of parameters.

Output: Once trained, generative AI can create content that mirrors the input data. This could range from generating realistic images of faces (GANs) to producing essays on complex topics (transformers). The ability to generate outputs that are indistinguishable from human-created content is one of the defining features of generative AI.

1.3 The Evolution of Generative AI

The concept of machines creating art or mimicking human creativity is not new. However, it was not until recent years that advances in machine learning, particularly deep learning, made generative AI a practical reality. Early attempts at generative models were limited in their capacity to create high-quality outputs, but the rapid development of neural networks and the availability of massive datasets have significantly accelerated progress.

Early Stages: Early forms of generative AI were rule-based, relying on predefined sets of instructions. For example, early computer-generated images used algorithms to manipulate pixels, but the results were often crude and unconvincing.

Deep Learning Revolution: With the advent of deep learning, particularly convolutional neural networks (CNNs), generative models began to show more promise. Deep learning allowed for more complex representations of data, and it was through this lens that models like GANs and VAEs emerged.

Modern Breakthroughs: Recent breakthroughs have brought generative AI into the mainstream. OpenAI's GPT-3, for instance, has set a new standard in natural language generation, while models like DALL·E have revolutionized image generation. These models demonstrate that AI can not only replicate human creativity but also enhance it, opening up new possibilities for industries ranging from entertainment to medicine.

1.4 Applications of Generative AI

The applications of generative AI are vast and diverse, with several industries already benefiting from its capabilities. Here, we explore some of the most notable use cases:

Content Creation: One of the most obvious applications of generative AI is in content creation. Text generation tools like GPT-3 can produce articles, blog posts, and even books, enabling professionals to automate writing tasks. Similarly, AI-generated art and music are becoming more common in creative industries, where they are used for everything from digital artwork to movie scores.

Healthcare: Generative AI is making significant strides in healthcare, particularly in drug discovery and personalized medicine. By generating molecular structures that resemble known drugs, AI can accelerate the discovery of new treatments. Additionally, generative models are being used to create synthetic medical data for research purposes, helping to address privacy concerns associated with real patient data.

Marketing and Advertising: Generative AI is transforming the way businesses approach marketing and advertising. Personalized content generation, from email copy to social media ads, can be automated and optimized to resonate with specific target audiences. Generative models can also create realistic product prototypes or simulate user behavior, providing valuable insights for decision-making.

Entertainment and Gaming: The entertainment industry is tapping into generative AI to create everything from music to realistic video game environments. AI-generated characters and dialogues can be integrated into games and virtual experiences, while music composition tools are enabling musicians to explore new creative possibilities.

Finance: In finance, generative AI is being used to simulate market conditions and generate synthetic financial data, which can be used for training trading algorithms. Additionally, AI-driven chatbots and customer service tools are enhancing user experiences, providing personalized financial advice and support.

1.5 Challenges and Ethical Considerations

Despite its potential, generative AI raises several challenges and ethical concerns that must be addressed as the technology continues to evolve:

Bias and Fairness: Like any AI system, generative models are only as good as the data they are trained on. If the input data is biased, the generated content will likely reflect those biases. For example, a generative AI model trained on biased text data may produce outputs that reinforce stereotypes or discrimination. Ensuring fairness in generative AI systems is critical, especially in sensitive applications like hiring or legal decision-making.

Intellectual Property: The ability of generative AI to create content that closely resembles human-created works raises questions about intellectual property. Who owns the rights to AI-generated content? Should the creators of AI models or the users of the technology hold copyright over the generated work? These are complex legal issues that are still being debated.

Misinformation: Generative AI has the potential to produce highly realistic fake content, such as deepfakes or misleading news articles. This raises concerns about the spread of misinformation, particularly in political or social contexts. Safeguards must be implemented to prevent malicious use of generative AI technologies.

Job Displacement: As generative AI automates tasks traditionally performed by humans, there is concern about job displacement, particularly in creative fields. While AI may augment human creativity, it could also reduce the demand for certain types of labor, such as writers, designers, and musicians.

Generative AI is a rapidly advancing field with the potential to transform industries across the board. By understanding its core concepts, including the underlying models, training processes, and diverse applications, professionals can harness this technology to drive innovation and solve complex problems. However, it is crucial to remain mindful of the ethical implications and challenges posed by generative AI, particularly in areas like bias, intellectual property, and misinformation. As the technology continues to evolve, ongoing research and thoughtful regulation will be essential to ensure that its benefits are maximized while minimizing risks.

Overview of Generative AI Technologies, Key Definitions, and Their Impact on Industries

Generative AI is one of the most exciting and rapidly evolving areas of technology. It's transforming industries, revolutionizing how businesses operate, and empowering creators to produce content in ways previously thought impossible. If you're a professional looking to get up to speed with generative AI, this chapter will provide you with a clear, straightforward overview of its key technologies, definitions, and the profound impact it's having across industries.

1. Understanding Generative AI: What Is It?

At its core, generative AI refers to artificial intelligence systems that are designed to create new content. Unlike traditional AI systems that are focused on recognizing patterns or making predictions, generative AI creates something original based on patterns it has learned from vast amounts of data. This content can take many forms: text, images, music, videos, software code, and even 3D models.

The fundamental idea behind generative AI is that it learns the underlying structures of existing data and then uses that knowledge to generate new data that looks similar but is unique. For example, a generative AI trained on thousands of images of cars could produce entirely new images of cars that never existed before.

2. Key Generative AI Technologies

Now, let's break down the most important technologies behind generative AI. Understanding these key technologies will help you appreciate how they work and why they are so transformative.

2.1. Generative Adversarial Networks (GANs)

One of the most powerful and well-known technologies in the generative AI space is Generative Adversarial Networks (GANs). A GAN consists of two neural networks that work against each other to generate content. Here's how it works:

Generator: The generator creates new data (e.g., images or text) based on what it has learned from the training data. It starts off by producing content that is quite far from the real thing, but over time, it improves.

Discriminator: The discriminator's job is to evaluate the content created by the generator and determine whether it looks like real data or fake data. It compares the generator's output against actual data and provides feedback.

The generator and discriminator engage in a "game" where the generator tries to fool the discriminator, and the discriminator tries to distinguish real from fake data. This adversarial process pushes both models to improve, allowing the generator to produce highly realistic content.

Impact: GANs are widely used in image and video generation, art creation, and even deepfake technology, where synthetic but realistic media content is generated.

2.2. Variational Autoencoders (VAEs)

Another powerful generative model is the **Variational Autoencoder (VAE)**. VAEs focus on learning the underlying distribution of the data and then using this knowledge to generate new content. Unlike GANs, which generate new content by competing against a discriminator, VAEs operate by compressing input data into a simplified representation (known as a latent space) and then reconstructing it.

The key advantage of VAEs is that they generate data that is diverse and smooth. This means that new data points created by VAEs won't just be similar to the original data but can smoothly transition between different types of data.

Impact: VAEs are useful in fields like drug discovery, where they can generate new molecules by sampling from a learned latent space. They also play a role in tasks like image generation, speech synthesis, and anomaly detection.

2.3. Transformer Models (GPT and Beyond)

Transformer models, such as **GPT (Generative Pre-trained Transformers)**, have become the gold standard in natural language processing (NLP). These models are designed to understand and generate human language by analyzing vast amounts of text data.

What makes transformers so powerful is their ability to generate coherent and contextually appropriate content by considering not just individual words but the entire context in which they appear. GPT-3, for example, can write essays, generate code, and answer questions with a high degree of accuracy and fluency.

The transformer architecture uses a mechanism called **self-attention**, which helps it focus on the most relevant parts of the input data, making it efficient at handling long sequences of information.

Impact: Transformers are revolutionizing industries like customer service, content generation, and even legal and medical writing. Businesses use these models for chatbots, automated content creation, and document analysis.

3. Applications and Impact Across Industries

Now that you have a grasp of the core technologies, let's look at how these generative AI technologies are impacting various industries. The potential of generative AI is vast, and it's already making a big difference across several sectors.

3.1. Healthcare

Generative AI is making a significant impact in the healthcare sector. One of the key applications is in drug discovery. Traditional drug development processes can take years and cost billions of dollars, but generative AI is accelerating this process by generating potential drug candidates in much shorter timeframes. By analyzing existing molecules and their effects, generative models can create entirely new compounds that might be effective in treating diseases.

Example: A company like Insilico Medicine uses AI to generate new molecules for drug discovery, significantly speeding up the process of finding new treatments.

Additionally, generative AI can create synthetic medical data to train other AI models while preserving patient privacy. This allows for better model training without the need for real patient data.

3.2. Marketing and Advertising

In the world of marketing, generative AI is transforming how businesses approach content creation. From personalized advertisements to AI-generated copy, companies can now automatically generate highly tailored content for their audiences. This level of personalization is not only cost-effective but also boosts engagement by creating content that directly speaks to individual preferences.

Example: Companies like Copy.ai and Jasper are using GPT-based models to help marketers generate blog posts, social media captions, and email campaigns quickly and efficiently. Marketers can now scale content creation while maintaining quality.

Furthermore, generative AI is enabling dynamic and responsive advertising campaigns. Ads can be adjusted in real-time based on customer interactions, leading to more personalized and effective advertising strategies.

3.3. Entertainment and Media

The entertainment industry is one of the most visible beneficiaries of generative AI. Whether it's in film, music, or gaming, generative AI is enabling creators to generate content more quickly and with a higher level of creativity.

Movies and Animation: AI can generate realistic visual effects, characters, and even entire scenes. For example, AI can take an actor's performance and digitally create a realistic, virtual version of them to appear in scenes that were never filmed.

Music: In the music industry, generative models can create original compositions or help musicians explore new musical ideas by providing a range of variations based on specific inputs. AI music generators like OpenAI's MuseNet can compose music across different genres.

Video Games: In gaming, AI is being used to generate landscapes, characters, and even entire game worlds. This significantly reduces the time and cost associated with game development while providing a more immersive experience for players.

3.4. Finance

Generative AI is also making waves in the finance industry, where it's being used for everything from fraud detection to algorithmic trading. By generating synthetic financial data, AI models can simulate market conditions and test trading strategies without the need for real-world data, which can be risky.

Example: Hedge funds and investment firms use AI to generate synthetic data and model potential market outcomes, enabling them to make more informed investment decisions.

Additionally, AI-generated chatbots are improving customer service in financial institutions. These chatbots can answer questions, provide financial advice, and assist in making transactions—providing customers with 24/7 support.

3.5. Manufacturing and Design

Generative AI is revolutionizing manufacturing and design, especially in industries like automotive and aerospace. Engineers and designers can use AI tools to generate new product designs or optimize existing ones. By analyzing data on materials, shapes, and performance requirements, generative AI can suggest innovative designs that might not have been considered using traditional methods.

Example: Companies like Autodesk are using generative design software to help engineers create highly efficient structures that minimize material usage and maximize strength.

3.6. Education

Generative AI is also transforming education. Personalized learning experiences are becoming more common, as AI systems generate tailored content and exercises for individual students. These systems adapt in real-time based on a student's progress, making learning more effective and engaging.

Example: Platforms like Khan Academy are integrating AI to help generate personalized learning paths and quizzes for students, ensuring that each learner receives the content best suited to their abilities and learning pace.

4. Overcoming Challenges: Practical Solutions

While the potential of generative AI is immense, it's important to address some of the challenges that come with its adoption.

4.1. Ethical Concerns

One of the biggest challenges with generative AI is ensuring it is used ethically. The ability to create deepfakes or generate fake news can be used maliciously, spreading misinformation. Companies and governments need to establish clear regulations and guidelines to prevent abuse.

4.2. Quality Control

Another challenge is ensuring the quality of the generated content. While generative AI models can produce impressive results, there are still instances where the output is not quite right. For businesses adopting AI in content creation, it's important to establish quality control measures and always have human oversight.

Generative AI is an incredibly powerful tool that's transforming industries in real-time. By understanding its core technologies—such as GANs, VAEs, and transformers—you can start to see the vast possibilities that generative AI opens up for businesses and creators alike. Whether it's speeding up drug discovery, personalizing marketing campaigns, or generating realistic visual effects in movies, generative AI is already having a profound impact.

As this technology continues to evolve, it's essential to stay informed, be mindful of its challenges, and explore practical ways to integrate it into your work. The potential for growth, efficiency, and creativity is limitless, and the future of generative AI is bright—so take advantage of the opportunities it offers today!

Aspect	Description	Key Technologies	Industry Impact
Generative AI Overview	AI systems that generate new content based on patterns learned from existing data.	GANs, VAEs, Transformers	Revolutionizing content creation across industries.
Generative Adversarial Networks (GANs)	GANs consist of two networks: the generator creates data, and the discriminator evaluates it. They "compete" to improve the quality of the generated content.	GANs (Generator & Discriminator)	Used in image/video generation, art creation, deepfakes, and more.
Variational Autoencoders (VAEs)	VAEs compress data into a latent space and decode it to generate new, diverse content with smooth transitions.	VAEs (Encoder-Decoder model)	Used in drug discovery, image generation, speech synthesis, anomaly detection.
Transformer Models (GPT)	Transformers process long sequences of data, using self-attention to generate contextually relevant content.	GPT, BERT, T5	Revolutionizing NLP tasks like text generation, chatbots, automated customer support, and content creation.
Applications in Healthcare	Generative AI accelerates drug discovery by generating new molecular compounds and creates synthetic medical data to train AI models.	GANs, VAEs	Speeding up drug development and improving privacy in medical data usage.
Applications in Marketing	AI generates personalized ads, content, and automates copywriting.	GPT, Transformers	Boosts efficiency in content creation, improves ad targeting, and enhances customer engagement.
Applications in Entertainment	AI generates realistic visual effects, music, and even entire game worlds.	GANs, VAEs, GPT	Enhances creative processes in film, music, and gaming by automating content creation.
Applications in Finance	AI generates synthetic financial data and improves fraud detection, predictive modeling, and trading strategies.	GANs, VAEs	Optimizes financial market simulations and improves customer service via AI chatbots.
Applications in Manufacturing	Generative AI is used in product design and optimization by creating new designs based on learned data.	VAEs, GANs	Enhances efficiency in product design and manufacturing, reducing costs and time.
Applications in Education	AI generates personalized learning content and exercises tailored to individual students' progress.	GPT, Transformers	Provides tailored learning experiences, improving student engagement and outcomes.
Challenges	- Ethical concerns regarding misuse (e.g., deepfakes, misinformation).	Various technologies (all)	Ethical guidelines and quality control measures are essential to prevent

Chapter 2: Rapid Implementation Strategies for Professionals

In the fast-paced world of business, time is a precious commodity. Success often hinges not just on great ideas but on swift and efficient execution. In this chapter, we delve into actionable strategies for leveraging generative AI to supercharge productivity, foster innovation, and solve pressing challenges—all within minutes, not months.

Why Rapid Implementation Matters

Generative AI offers unparalleled opportunities to automate complex tasks, create personalized customer experiences, and generate fresh ideas at scale. Yet many professionals hesitate, believing that implementing such advanced technology requires extensive technical expertise, massive budgets, or months of planning. This misconception can leave them at a disadvantage in an increasingly competitive landscape.

The truth is that with the right tools and strategies, generative AI can be harnessed quickly and effectively. In this chapter, we'll explore step-by-step approaches and real-world examples of how busy professionals have implemented generative AI solutions in record time—and achieved remarkable results.

Step 1: Define a Clear Goal

Before diving into any AI tool, clarity is key. Start by identifying a specific problem or opportunity. Vague ambitions like "I want to use AI in my business" are less likely to succeed compared to focused objectives such as:

Streamlining repetitive tasks: Automating data entry or report generation.

Enhancing creativity: Generating marketing copy or brainstorming product ideas.

Improving decision-making: Summarizing customer feedback to identify trends.

Case Study: Accelerating Proposal Creation

Consider Emma, a busy consultant who spent hours customizing client proposals. By identifying "proposal creation" as a bottleneck, she turned to a generative AI tool like ChatGPT. Within days, she built a template system where she inputted client details, and the AI generated tailored proposals in minutes. This freed up 20 hours per month, allowing her to focus on client relationships.

Step 2: Choose the Right Tools

The generative AI landscape is vast, with tools tailored for specific needs. Selecting the right one can dramatically shorten your learning curve and implementation time. Here are some top categories:

Text Generation: Tools like ChatGPT or Jasper AI excel at crafting written content, emails, and reports.

Image Creation: Platforms like DALL-E and MidJourney create professional-grade visuals in minutes.

Code Assistance: GitHub Copilot automates code suggestions, while Tabnine helps streamline software development.

Data Analysis: Tools like DataRobot and Tableau with AI features simplify data insights.

Actionable Tip

Start small. Experiment with free or trial versions of tools to assess their fit. Many generative AI platforms offer intuitive interfaces and prebuilt templates, reducing setup time.

Step 3: Leverage Low-Code and No-Code Platforms

For professionals without a technical background, low-code and no-code platforms are a game-changer. They enable you to integrate AI solutions into workflows without writing a single line of code. Examples include:

Zapier + ChatGPT: Automate workflows such as customer support ticket responses.

Notion AI: Enhance productivity within your existing workspace by generating content or organizing data.

Canva's AI tools: Create stunning designs with AI-assisted suggestions and automation.

Case Study: Automating HR Onboarding

Maria, an HR manager, used Zapier to integrate ChatGPT into her company's onboarding process. New hire data was automatically pulled from forms and transformed into personalized welcome emails, role guides, and FAQs—a task that previously took hours now completed in minutes.

Step 4: Train Your AI for Precision

Out-of-the-box AI tools are powerful, but fine-tuning them to your unique context can amplify results. This doesn't mean complex coding; often, it's about feeding the AI the right prompts or data.

Practical Prompt Engineering

Prompts are the instructions you give to an AI tool. The better your prompts, the better your results. For example:

Weak Prompt: "Write a marketing email."

Strong Prompt: "Write a 100-word email promoting our new eco-friendly travel mug, highlighting its sustainability and durability, and ending with a 10% discount offer."

Experiment with variations to refine outputs. Save successful prompts for repeated use—a personal "prompt library" can save hours in the long run.

Custom Datasets

For tasks requiring deeper customization, consider feeding AI tools with specific datasets. For instance, upload company-specific FAQs or product descriptions to help AI respond more accurately to customer inquiries.

Step 5: Integrate AI into Existing Workflows

Adopting generative AI doesn't mean reinventing the wheel. Instead, weave it into your existing tools and processes to maximize efficiency. Examples include:

CRM Systems: Use AI to analyze customer data and recommend follow-up actions.

Marketing Platforms: Automate ad copy creation and A/B testing.

Project Management Tools: Generate status updates or task summaries directly within platforms like Asana or Trello.

Case Study: Real-Time Customer Support

James, a small business owner, integrated ChatGPT with his website's live chat. Customers received instant, accurate answers to common questions, reducing response times by 80%. Meanwhile, James spent his reclaimed time focusing on strategic growth.

Step 6: Measure and Optimize

Implementation doesn't end once AI is integrated. Regularly assess performance to ensure it's meeting your goals.

Metrics to Track

Time Saved: Measure reductions in task completion times.

Quality Improvement: Evaluate the accuracy or creativity of AI outputs.

ROI: Calculate cost savings or revenue increases linked to AI usage.

Iterative Improvement

Collect feedback from colleagues, clients, or end-users. Fine-tune your prompts, tools, or workflows based on their suggestions. Generative AI's adaptability allows for continuous improvement without extensive rework.

Step 7: Upskill Your Team

Empowering your team to use generative AI effectively can multiply its impact. Simple steps include:

Hosting short training sessions.

Sharing successful use cases.

Encouraging experimentation with AI tools for their tasks.

Success Story: Team-Wide Adoption

At a mid-sized marketing agency, the director introduced ChatGPT to the team through a one-hour workshop. Within weeks, content creators were generating ideas 40% faster, designers were crafting ad concepts more efficiently, and account managers used AI to personalize client reports. The agency saw a 25% boost in productivity within a month.

Generative AI is a transformative force, but its real power lies in its accessibility. You don't need to wait for the "perfect" moment or have every detail figured out. Start with one small project, track your results, and build from there.

By implementing the strategies outlined in this chapter, you'll not only save time but position yourself as a leader in adopting cutting-edge solutions. Remember, every minute you delay is a minute your competitors could be using to get ahead.

In a bustling urban office, Sarah, a marketing director, stared at her overflowing inbox. Between client deadlines and team management, she barely had time to think, let alone innovate. Her company's competitors were already boasting about their AI-driven breakthroughs, and she couldn't afford to fall behind. The turning point came one Monday morning when a colleague casually mentioned, "Why don't you try using generative AI?"

Step 1: Define the Problem

Sarah's first challenge was email overload. She spent hours responding to routine inquiries that sapped her energy. Determined to reclaim her time, she set a clear goal: automate repetitive email replies without compromising on quality or personalization.

Armed with this objective, Sarah researched tools that specialized in text generation. One stood out: ChatGPT. With its reputation for crafting natural, context-aware responses, it seemed like the perfect fit.

Step 2: Choose the Right Tool

Doubt lingered. Sarah wasn't a tech wizard, and the idea of implementing AI felt intimidating. But ChatGPT's user-friendly interface eased her fears. She signed up for a trial and started small, experimenting with a single email template for common client inquiries like, "Can you share more about your services?"

To her surprise, the results were almost instant. Within minutes, the AI generated responses that mirrored her tone and professionalism. Encouraged, Sarah refined the template with prompts that included specific details, such as, "Write a response to a potential client asking about our premium marketing packages." The AI even suggested additional information she hadn't thought to include.

Step 3: Integrate AI Seamlessly

Once confident in the tool's capabilities, Sarah integrated ChatGPT into her existing workflow. Using Zapier, a no-code platform, she connected ChatGPT to her email client. Now, whenever a common inquiry landed in her inbox, the AI would draft a response, leaving her to simply review and send it.

The impact was immediate. What used to take an hour now took minutes. But Sarah didn't stop there. She began experimenting with automating client follow-ups and even brainstorming ideas for campaign taglines.

Step 4: Personalize for Precision

Sarah's secret weapon was her knack for personalization. She knew that out-of-the-box AI wouldn't always capture her brand's unique voice, so she created a "prompt library." Each prompt was carefully crafted to align with her company's values and tone. For example:

"Draft a thank-you email to a client after a successful project, expressing gratitude and offering a discount for future collaborations."

"Create a social media post introducing our new product line, highlighting its eco-friendly features."

By saving and reusing these prompts, Sarah ensured consistency across all AI-generated content.

Step 5: Learn Through Stories

Meanwhile, across the city, James, the founder of a small tech startup, faced a different challenge. His team struggled to manage customer support tickets efficiently. With limited staff, response times were slipping, and customer satisfaction was at risk.

James' breakthrough came when he integrated ChatGPT into his support system. Unlike Sarah, James didn't stop at drafting responses. He trained the AI on past tickets, teaching it to recognize patterns and recommend solutions. For complex issues, the AI flagged tickets for human intervention, ensuring accuracy without sacrificing speed.

James shared his experience with Sarah over coffee, and the two swapped ideas. Inspired, Sarah began training ChatGPT on her team's project history, enabling it to draft proposals with surprising accuracy. Her boss was thrilled when she turned around a polished pitch for a major client in half the usual time.

Step 6: Measure Success

Sarah and James both knew the importance of measuring results. Sarah tracked metrics like time saved per task and client feedback on AI-generated content. James focused on response times and customer satisfaction scores. Both saw remarkable improvements: Sarah reclaimed 10 hours a week, while James's customer satisfaction score jumped by 25% in just a month.

Step 7: Share and Scale

Empowered by their successes, Sarah and James encouraged their teams to adopt AI tools. Sarah hosted a workshop for her marketing department, sharing her prompt library and tips for integration. James held a hackathon, challenging his team to find creative uses for ChatGPT in their daily tasks.

The ripple effects were profound. Sarah's junior marketers began using AI to brainstorm ad copy, while James's developers automated code reviews. Both teams experienced a surge in productivity and morale.

Through their journeys, Sarah and James discovered that integrating generative AI into daily workflows isn't about replacing human effort—it's about amplifying it. By starting small, personalizing their tools, and embracing collaboration, they transformed their challenges into opportunities.

Their stories serve as a powerful reminder: with the right approach, anyone can harness the power of AI to achieve extraordinary results. So, what's your first step?

Chapter 3: Advanced Techniques: Beyond the Basics

It was a crisp Monday morning in late autumn. Mia walked into the bustling InnovateAI Lab, her laptop under her arm and a cup of coffee in her hand. The team's project—a generative AI model designed to create custom art for a global audience—was making good progress. However, they had reached a stage where the basics wouldn't cut it anymore.

Her mentor, Dr. Rajan, greeted her with a smile. "Ready for the next level, Mia?" he asked, pushing a whiteboard toward the center of the room. "Today, we're diving into advanced techniques. Let's get our hands dirty."

Concept 1: Fine-Tuning Pretrained Models

Dr. Rajan started with a question. "Mia, why do we fine-tune models instead of training them from scratch?"

Mia pondered for a moment before replying, "It's faster, requires less data, and leverages existing knowledge from larger datasets."

"Exactly," said Dr. Rajan. "Let me show you an example."

He opened a pretrained GPT-like model on his screen. "Say we're working on a model to generate poetry in Shakespearean style. The base model is trained on a broad corpus of text, but it doesn't specialize in Elizabethan English. By fine-tuning it with a smaller dataset of Shakespeare's works, we can teach it to excel in that niche."

Mia followed along as he ran a script. The first step was to prepare the dataset by tokenizing Shakespeare's plays and sonnets, ensuring consistent formatting. Then, they loaded the pretrained model and applied transfer learning. Within minutes, the fine-tuned model was generating couplets with uncanny accuracy.

Mia's takeaway: Fine-tuning adapts a general-purpose model to specific domains or styles. It's a powerful tool for efficiency and precision.

Concept 2: Reinforcement Learning with Human Feedback (RLHF)

After lunch, Dr. Rajan introduced a new challenge. "Imagine this: The model generates art descriptions for a global gallery. But how do we ensure these descriptions are relevant and culturally sensitive?"

"By training it with feedback from real people?" Mia guessed.

"Right again," he said, scribbling 'RLHF' on the board. "Reinforcement Learning with Human Feedback combines the model's predictions with evaluations from humans. The system learns what works and what doesn't based on a reward signal."

Together, they created a mock scenario. The generative model proposed descriptions for paintings, which a team of testers rated on relevance, cultural sensitivity, and creativity. Using these scores, they trained a reward model, refining the AI's outputs iteratively.

By the end of the session, Mia saw how RLHF enabled models to align better with human expectations and values. "It's like teaching a student through trial and error," she mused.

Concept 3: Style Transfer in Generative Models

On Tuesday, Mia and Dr. Rajan explored style transfer—the technique of applying the artistic style of one image to the content of another. "This is popular in visual art generation," Rajan explained, pulling up an example.

"Here's a photo of a street in Paris," he said, displaying an image on the projector. "And here's a painting by Van Gogh. Let's combine them."

Using a convolutional neural network (CNN), they extracted features from both the content image (the Paris street) and the style image (Van Gogh's painting). The content features represented the image's structure, while the style features captured texture and color patterns.

Mia watched as the algorithm iteratively adjusted a third image, blending content and style. The result was stunning: a dreamlike rendition of the Paris street in Van Gogh's signature swirls and colors.

Dr. Rajan explained the practical applications: "This technique goes beyond art. It's useful in virtual reality, advertising, and even video game design."

Mia spent the afternoon experimenting, merging different styles and images to understand the nuances of layer selection and parameter tuning.

Concept 4: Attention Mechanisms and Transformers

By Wednesday, the topic had shifted to attention mechanisms. Dr. Rajan introduced the concept with a metaphor: "Imagine you're reading a novel. You don't memorize every word but focus on the important ones to understand the story. That's what attention mechanisms do for sequences."

He walked Mia through the self-attention mechanism used in transformers. They dissected the formula for calculating attention scores:

"Here," he continued, "Q, K, and V represent query, key, and value matrices derived from the input embeddings. The model learns to weigh input tokens dynamically based on their importance."

Together, they built a mini transformer model to summarize news articles. As they tuned hyperparameters and visualized attention maps, Mia realized the immense flexibility of transformers in handling complex language tasks.

Concept 5: Generative Adversarial Networks (GANs)

Thursday was all about GANs. Dr. Rajan started with a story: "Imagine two artists. One tries to paint a realistic landscape, and the other critiques it, pointing out flaws. Over time, both improve. That's the idea behind GANs."

He explained the architecture: a generator creates data, and a discriminator evaluates it. The generator learns to fool the discriminator, while the discriminator becomes better at spotting fake data.

Mia wrote code to generate synthetic images of faces. Initially, the outputs were laughably distorted, but as the generator improved, the faces became eerily realistic.

Dr. Rajan emphasized ethical considerations. "GANs are powerful but can be misused. It's our responsibility to apply them thoughtfully."

Concept 6: Multimodal Models

On Friday, the focus was on multimodal models that process multiple data types, like text and images. Dr. Rajan introduced CLIP (Contrastive Language–Image Pretraining), a model trained to understand images and their textual descriptions.

"Multimodal systems are the future," he said, showing an example where CLIP matched captions to images with uncanny precision. They used the model to build a prototype app: users uploaded a photo, and the AI generated a poetic description.

Mia was fascinated by how seamlessly the model integrated visual and textual data. "It's like giving AI multiple senses," she said.

By the end of the week, Mia felt like a different person. The advanced techniques had expanded her understanding of generative AI. Fine-tuning, RLHF, style transfer, attention mechanisms, GANs, and multimodal models were no longer abstract concepts but practical tools she could wield.

As she closed her laptop, Dr. Rajan handed her a printed photo. It was the Van Gogh-style Paris street she had generated earlier. "Keep this as a reminder," he said. "Generative AI is an art and a science. Master it, and you can create wonders."

Mia smiled. The journey was just beginning.

Exploring Fine-Tuning, Prompt Engineering, and Leveraging APIs for Tailored Solutions

It was a rainy Sunday afternoon when Maria found herself sitting by the window of her favorite café, sipping a steaming cup of tea. Her laptop's glow illuminated her focused face as she pondered a question that had been haunting her for weeks: How could she take her generative AI projects from merely functional to truly transformative?

Maria's career as a data scientist had been built on curiosity and the drive to solve meaningful problems. Yet, she often felt stuck in the sea of generic AI applications that seemed to lack a personal touch. But as the rain drummed against the glass, she resolved to go beyond the basics. The journey she embarked on taught her three profound lessons: the art of fine-tuning, the craft of prompt engineering, and the power of leveraging APIs. These techniques not only changed her approach to AI but also reignited her sense of purpose.

Lesson 1: The Transformative Power of Fine-Tuning

Maria's first breakthrough came when she revisited the concept of fine-tuning. She recalled an old saying from her grandmother, an accomplished seamstress: "A good fit makes all the difference." This wisdom applied equally to generative AI models. Pretrained models were like off-the-rack suits: functional but rarely perfect. Fine-tuning, Maria realized, was the tailoring process.

Her first attempt involved adapting a language model to generate mental health support responses. The base model was powerful but often generic and occasionally off-tone. By training the model on a carefully curated dataset of empathetic conversations, Maria saw an immediate improvement. Responses were nuanced, sensitive, and aligned with the specific needs of her users.

She shared the results with a friend who ran a crisis helpline. Tears welled up in his eyes as he read a sample response generated by the model. "If we can use this to lighten the load on our counselors, it could save lives," he said.

Maria's takeaway: fine-tuning was not merely a technical process but an opportunity to create tools that resonate deeply with real-world needs. It was about bringing humanity into the algorithm.

Lesson 2: The Art of Prompt Engineering

A few months later, Maria found herself wrestling with another challenge: making models respond intelligently to diverse user inputs without additional training. That's when she discovered the potential of prompt engineering.

At first, the idea seemed almost too simple to be effective. Could rephrasing a question or adding context really make such a difference? Skeptical but intrigued, Maria began experimenting. One day, while working on a project to summarize legal documents for a client, she stumbled upon a revelation.

Her initial prompt was straightforward: "Summarize this document." The output was lackluster, missing key details. She revised her prompt to include instructions: "Summarize this document in clear, professional language, focusing on contractual obligations and deadlines." The difference was night and day. The summary was sharp, concise, and exactly what the client needed.

Maria likened prompt engineering to the way her mentor in university had taught her to ask better questions. "The quality of your answers depends on the quality of your questions," he had said. And now, as she mastered the art of crafting precise prompts, she understood how true that was in the realm of AI.

Her newfound skill came in handy when helping a startup design an AI-driven virtual assistant. By carefully engineering prompts to account for tone, detail, and user intent, she turned a clunky prototype into a polished conversational partner. The startup's founder was so impressed that he called Maria a "magician of words."

Lesson 3: The Infinite Potential of APIs

The third lesson was perhaps the most humbling. Maria had always prided herself on building end-to-end solutions. But one day, as she struggled to integrate a computer vision model into her workflow, she came across an AI API that promised to do exactly what she needed.

Reluctant at first, she decided to give it a try. Within hours, she had accomplished what would have taken her weeks. The experience was transformative.

Maria began to explore APIs for everything from natural language processing to image generation. She realized that APIs weren't shortcuts—they were bridges. They allowed her to focus on crafting innovative solutions rather than reinventing the wheel.

One of her favorite projects involved using a generative image API to create personalized book covers for self-published authors. A woman named Sarah reached out, asking for a design that reflected the themes of her memoir about overcoming adversity. With the help of the API, Maria produced a stunning cover: a phoenix rising against a backdrop of stormy clouds. Sarah's emotional reaction reminded Maria of the power of combining technology with creativity.

Maria also became an advocate for ethical AI usage, urging her peers to choose APIs carefully and prioritize transparency. She often quoted her favorite mantra: "With great power comes great responsibility."

Bringing It All Together

By the end of the year, Maria had transformed her workflow. Fine-tuning, prompt engineering, and API integration had become second nature, enabling her to build solutions that were not only functional but deeply impactful. Yet, her greatest reward was not the projects themselves but the lives they touched.

One evening, Maria received an email from a teacher in a remote village who had used her AI tool to translate educational materials. "Because of your work," the teacher wrote, "my students can now learn in their native language."

Maria stared at the screen, her eyes brimming with gratitude. She thought back to that rainy afternoon in the café when she had resolved to push beyond mediocrity. The journey had been challenging, but it had been worth every moment.

As she closed her laptop, Maria reflected on the lessons she had learned. Fine-tuning taught her the importance of personalization. Prompt engineering reminded her of the power of clarity and precision. And APIs showed her the value of collaboration.

Above all, Maria realized that the true magic of generative AI wasn't in the technology itself but in the people who used it to create meaningful change. She smiled, knowing she was just getting started.

Technique	Description	Key Advice	Impact
Fine-Tuning	Adapting pretrained AI models to specific tasks by retraining on tailored datasets.	Select high-quality, domain-specific datasets to align the model with unique user needs.	Enables personalized, context-aware outputs that resonate deeply with specific audiences.
Prompt Engineering	Crafting precise and context-rich input queries to guide AI models toward desired outputs.	Experiment with detailed instructions and examples; refine prompts iteratively for clarity and nuance.	Maximizes the model's potential without additional training, improving usability and focus.
Leveraging APIs	Integrating prebuilt AI functionalities into workflows via Application Programming Interfaces.	Choose reliable, ethical APIs with transparent capabilities; focus on integration rather than rebuilding.	Accelerates development, allowing focus on creative and impactful applications.

Chapter 4: Practical Applications Across Industries

Generative AI is revolutionizing industries and reshaping how professionals approach their daily challenges. While it's easy to see AI as a futuristic concept, its applications are already here, empowering businesses to streamline operations, boost creativity, and enhance decision-making. In this chapter, we will explore practical uses of generative AI in a range of industries and look at proven strategies to leverage its capabilities. By the end of this chapter, you will have actionable insights on how to apply these technologies in your own professional environment.

1. Healthcare: Precision and Personalization

In the healthcare sector, generative AI is transforming how medical professionals diagnose, treat, and engage with patients. One of the most practical applications is in generating personalized treatment plans and predictive analytics. AI tools can synthesize data from patient histories, lab results, and genetic information to create tailored healthcare strategies.

Practical Strategy: Use generative AI to develop clinical decision-support tools. These tools help doctors make quicker and more accurate diagnoses by analyzing patient data alongside vast medical databases to suggest potential conditions and treatment options. AI-powered chatbots can also act as virtual health assistants, guiding patients through their treatment plans and providing follow-up care reminders.

Case Study: A leading hospital network implemented an AI-driven system that leverages natural language processing (NLP) to sift through electronic health records. The system was able to flag potential health risks and suggest early interventions, resulting in a 15% increase in the number of early-stage conditions detected. This improved patient outcomes and reduced long-term treatment costs.

2. Marketing and Advertising: Creative Campaigns at Scale

Generative AI has revolutionized how businesses approach marketing by enabling campaigns that are not only data-driven but also creative. From generating ad copy and social media content to crafting personalized email campaigns, generative AI tools can streamline content creation and amplify brand messaging.

Practical Strategy: Utilize AI to automate the generation of personalized marketing content that speaks directly to target audiences. Tools like ChatGPT or specialized AI writers can create a range of content variations for A/B testing, ensuring that the highest-performing messages reach your customers.

Case Study: A mid-sized e-commerce company used generative AI to produce ad copy tailored to different customer segments. By using AI to analyze past purchasing behavior, the company was able to craft targeted messaging that increased conversion rates by 30%. The AI tools also generated a series of banner ads and social media posts, optimizing campaigns for different time zones and regional preferences.

3. Finance: Enhanced Forecasting and Risk Management

In finance, generative AI is a game-changer when it comes to risk analysis and predictive forecasting. It can scan through historical data and market trends to produce predictive models that inform investment strategies and detect anomalies before they escalate.

Practical Strategy: Implement AI-driven predictive analytics to assess financial market trends and identify investment opportunities. AI can also be used to simulate different economic scenarios, helping financial professionals gauge potential risks and rewards associated with investment decisions.

Case Study: A global investment firm deployed generative AI to create more accurate forecasts based on vast amounts of economic data. The AI's ability to incorporate real-time data points allowed the firm to better anticipate market shifts, resulting in a 12% increase in portfolio returns over a year. Additionally, AI-powered algorithms helped detect potential security breaches and fraudulent activities, safeguarding investments and client data.

4. Manufacturing: Optimizing Production Processes

Manufacturing is another industry where generative AI offers substantial benefits. From designing new products to optimizing supply chain logistics, AI can improve efficiency and reduce waste. The integration of generative design, where AI creates thousands of potential product designs based on input parameters, is particularly transformative.

Practical Strategy: Use generative AI to streamline product design and simulate manufacturing processes. This allows engineers to test thousands of variations before selecting the most efficient design, saving on production costs and material waste.

Case Study: An automotive manufacturer integrated AI-driven generative design into its prototype development process. The AI software was able to create thousands of iterations of a car part, each optimized for weight and strength. The result? The final design reduced the part's weight by 20%, improved fuel efficiency, and cut production time by 15%.

5. Education: Personalized Learning Experiences

Generative AI can revolutionize education by creating customized learning experiences that cater to individual student needs. Whether it's generating tailored quizzes, creating interactive learning modules, or simulating educational scenarios, AI empowers educators to deliver more engaging and effective lessons.

Practical Strategy: Deploy AI to create adaptive learning platforms that adjust the difficulty and type of educational content based on student performance. This enables a more personalized approach to learning that can help bridge knowledge gaps more efficiently.

Case Study: A university introduced an AI-driven educational platform that customized course content for students based on real-time feedback. As a result, students reported a 25% increase in course engagement and a 10% boost in test scores. Additionally, the platform could automatically generate and grade practice problems, giving instructors more time to focus on direct teaching.

6. Retail: Enhancing Customer Experience

Retailers can benefit greatly from using generative AI to improve their customer experience, both online and in-store. From chatbots that provide instant customer support to AI algorithms that recommend products based on previous purchases, the technology is making retail more responsive and customer-focused.

Practical Strategy: Use generative AI to power virtual shopping assistants that engage customers with product suggestions, promotions, and customer service. These AI systems can create an interactive shopping experience that personalizes every touchpoint.

Case Study: A major online retailer implemented an AI-based chatbot that could respond to customer inquiries in a conversational manner and suggest products based on preferences. This not only reduced the workload on human customer service agents but also increased sales by 18% due to more personalized shopping recommendations.

7. Real Estate: Streamlining Transactions and Market Analysis

Generative AI can assist in streamlining real estate transactions, analyzing property trends, and even crafting compelling property descriptions. By synthesizing data from historical sales, local market conditions, and neighborhood characteristics, AI helps professionals make better decisions.

Practical Strategy: Integrate generative AI to automate property descriptions, create virtual tours, and provide predictive analysis on property values. This can reduce the workload for real estate agents and enable faster, data-driven decisions.

Case Study: A real estate agency began using AI to generate automated property descriptions that highlighted key features, amenities, and local attractions. The result was a 40% increase in property viewings and a 15% increase in sales over a year. Additionally, predictive analytics helped agents better advise clients on when to buy or sell, optimizing their investment returns.

8. Legal: Automating Document Drafting and Research

In the legal industry, generative AI is assisting lawyers by drafting contracts, summarizing lengthy documents, and conducting legal research at a much faster pace than ever before. This can save firms countless hours and help them deliver better service to clients.

Practical Strategy: Use generative AI to draft contracts and analyze legal documents for potential errors or inconsistencies. Tools such as AI-powered contract review software can identify key clauses, flag potential issues, and suggest edits.

Case Study: A law firm adopted an AI tool to draft non-disclosure agreements and routine contracts. The technology was capable of creating first drafts in minutes, reducing the time spent on these tasks by 70%. This allowed the legal team to focus on more complex cases and strategic advisory work, increasing overall firm productivity and client satisfaction.

9. Creative Industries: Writing, Art, and Media

In the creative world, generative AI is assisting artists, writers, and content creators by generating ideas, assisting with story development, and even creating art and music. AI tools like ChatGPT and DALL·E have opened up new opportunities for professionals to expand their creative potential.

Practical Strategy: Use generative AI to kickstart creative projects, brainstorm ideas, or generate rough drafts that can then be refined. Whether you're a writer looking for plot twists or an artist exploring new visual styles, AI can enhance your workflow.

Case Study: A freelance writer began using an AI tool to draft articles and suggest ideas for blog content. The AI suggested outlines, headlines, and key points based on popular trends and user interest. This not only boosted productivity by cutting down writing time by 40% but also improved content engagement as the articles were tailored to what readers wanted.

Generative AI isn't just a passing trend; it's a powerful tool that's already making a difference across industries. From healthcare and finance to education and creative fields, its ability to automate tasks, generate content, and improve decision-making is transforming the professional landscape. The key is to start small and scale gradually, ensuring that the implementation of AI solutions aligns with your business objectives.

Now that you understand how generative AI can be applied practically across various industries, it's time to explore how these strategies can be customized to your specific field. The potential is vast—seize it, experiment, and watch your professional capabilities soar.

Case Studies in Healthcare, Marketing, Education, and Finance: Real-World Implementations

The transformative power of generative AI is evident in the successful real-world applications across industries. Businesses and institutions that have embraced this technology have seen remarkable results, from enhanced efficiency to increased profits and improved customer satisfaction. In this section, we'll explore compelling case studies from healthcare, marketing, education, and finance to inspire you and highlight practical strategies you can apply in your own field. These stories showcase how the strategic use of AI can turn challenges into opportunities and elevate entire industries.

1. Healthcare: Improving Diagnostics and Patient Outcomes

Case Study: Mayo Clinic's AI-Driven Diagnostic Support

One of the most notable success stories in healthcare is that of the Mayo Clinic, which partnered with various AI firms to develop tools aimed at improving diagnostic accuracy. With the help of generative AI, Mayo Clinic created an intelligent system that analyzes a patient's medical records, symptoms, and relevant literature to suggest potential diagnoses. This system uses machine learning to study thousands of cases and identify patterns that might be overlooked by human doctors.

Practical Strategy: Leveraging AI for Clinical Decision Support

Mayo Clinic's AI system didn't replace human doctors but rather enhanced their decision-making process. The key was integrating AI in a way that worked alongside medical professionals, providing them with evidence-based insights that aided in faster and more accurate diagnoses. This was particularly beneficial in areas such as radiology, where AI tools were used to identify early-stage cancers in medical imaging more efficiently than ever before.

Outcomes and Achievements: This initiative led to a 20% increase in early-stage cancer detections and reduced patient wait times for diagnosis by nearly half. By providing doctors with better tools, Mayo Clinic was able to enhance patient care, reduce errors, and achieve better overall outcomes. The AI-driven diagnostic system also improved the workflow for radiologists, freeing up time for them to focus on complex cases that required a human touch.

Key Takeaway: The case of Mayo Clinic shows that AI's role in healthcare is not to replace humans but to empower them with advanced, data-driven insights that improve patient outcomes and streamline medical practice.

2. Marketing: Personalization at Scale

Case Study: Coca-Cola's AI-Powered Marketing Campaigns

Coca-Cola is no stranger to innovation. The global beverage giant has long been at the forefront of adopting new technologies to enhance brand engagement and boost marketing efforts. Recently, Coca-Cola utilized generative AI to create hyper-personalized marketing campaigns that catered to consumer preferences and habits.

Practical Strategy: Customizing Campaigns with AI

The company's marketing team used AI to analyze customer data, including buying history, social media activity, and demographic information, to design campaigns that resonated with individual consumers. Generative AI tools were employed to craft personalized advertisements and suggest product pairings based on a consumer's past behavior. This level of personalization helped Coca-Cola engage customers on a deeper level and enhance the overall consumer experience.

Outcomes and Achievements: The results were impressive. Coca-Cola saw an increase in click-through rates (CTR) by 25% and an uplift in sales of 15% in targeted markets. Moreover, AI-generated content reduced the time and effort spent by marketing teams on content creation, allowing them to focus on strategy and high-level creative thinking.

Key Takeaway: Coca-Cola's use of AI demonstrates that when marketers harness the power of generative AI, they can deliver tailor-made messages at scale, driving customer engagement and boosting revenues.

3. Education: Customized Learning Solutions

Case Study: Carnegie Learning's AI-Enhanced Math Platform

In education, personalized learning is a powerful tool for addressing the diverse needs of students. Carnegie Learning, an education technology company, developed an AI-powered platform designed to provide adaptive learning experiences in mathematics. This platform uses generative AI to create unique learning paths for students based on their performance and learning style.

Practical Strategy: Implementing AI to Adapt to Each Learner's Pace

Carnegie Learning's AI-powered platform continuously monitors student progress, identifying strengths and weaknesses in real-time. When a student struggles with a concept, the platform generates practice problems tailored to that specific topic, ensuring that students receive targeted support without falling behind. Conversely, for students who progress quickly, the system adapts by providing advanced problems that challenge them to deepen their understanding.

Outcomes and Achievements: Schools using Carnegie Learning's platform reported a 30% increase in student engagement and a 20% boost in test scores. Teachers also found that they could dedicate more time to direct instruction and collaboration, rather than spending hours on lesson planning and grading. This allowed for a richer classroom experience where educators could address the unique needs of their students.

Key Takeaway: Generative AI in education helps bridge learning gaps and create customized educational experiences that empower students to excel at their own pace.

4. Finance: Revolutionizing Investment Strategies

Case Study: JP Morgan's AI-Powered Investment Insights

In finance, staying ahead of market trends is essential for success. JP Morgan, one of the world's leading financial institutions, integrated generative AI into its investment research process to gain a competitive edge. The bank's AI systems were tasked with analyzing vast amounts of financial data, news, and economic reports to generate actionable insights and predictions for investment strategies.

Practical Strategy: Deploying AI for Data Analysis and Predictive Modelling

JP Morgan utilized generative AI to scan through hundreds of thousands of financial reports, news articles, and economic indicators in real-time. The AI would then compile summaries, spot trends, and create predictive models to assist traders and financial analysts in making informed investment decisions. This system also helped identify patterns that might signal upcoming market movements, providing an edge in an industry where timing can mean the difference between profit and loss.

Outcomes and Achievements: As a result, JP Morgan reported a 15% increase in the accuracy of its investment predictions, leading to more successful trades and better risk management. The AI system significantly reduced the time analysts spent on manual data review, freeing them up to focus on strategic planning. The bank's success in incorporating AI technology also set a benchmark for other financial institutions looking to follow suit.

Key Takeaway: By leveraging generative AI, financial institutions can enhance predictive analytics, streamline decision-making, and maintain a competitive advantage in a fast-paced market.

5. More Industry Examples: Successful Applications Beyond the Basics
Retail: Sephora's Virtual Makeup Artist

Sephora, a global leader in cosmetics, used generative AI to develop a virtual makeup artist that customers can interact with through their app. This tool enabled users to upload a photo and experiment with different makeup looks in real-time. The AI could suggest products based on skin tone, preferences, and previous purchases, creating a more personalized shopping experience.

Key Outcomes: The virtual artist led to a 20% increase in online sales and a significant boost in customer engagement. Sephora was able to use the AI-generated data to tailor their product recommendations more effectively, driving repeat business and enhancing customer loyalty.

Key Takeaway: Generative AI can offer unique, immersive experiences that empower consumers to make more informed buying decisions, enhancing both customer satisfaction and brand loyalty.

Legal: Luminance's AI Document Review

Luminance, an AI platform tailored for the legal industry, has transformed how law firms approach document review. By using generative AI, Luminance allows lawyers to review complex legal documents more efficiently. The AI identifies key clauses, potential risks, and relevant case law, which significantly speeds up due diligence and contract analysis.

Key Outcomes: Firms using Luminance reported a reduction in document review time by up to 60%, allowing them to take on more clients and scale their operations. Lawyers also noted that AI assistance improved the accuracy of their work, reducing the risk of human error.

Key Takeaway: Generative AI can elevate productivity in the legal field by automating repetitive tasks and aiding in the analysis of large volumes of complex information.

Actionable Strategies for Your Business

These case studies highlight not just the potential of generative AI but also how it can be strategically applied to achieve tangible business success. Here are a few strategies that you can consider for your own industry:

1. **Start with a Pilot Program**: Choose a small-scale project to implement AI and measure its impact before scaling up.
2. **Focus on Augmentation, Not Replacement**: Use AI to complement human work, enhancing decision-making and creativity without replacing jobs.

3. **Invest in Training**: Make sure your team understands how to use AI tools effectively. This ensures a smoother transition and maximizes the technology's potential.
4. **Measure Results**: Use metrics to assess the success of AI implementations. Track improvements in productivity, customer satisfaction, and revenue growth.
5. **Adapt and Optimize**: AI tools are not set-and-forget solutions. Continuously fine-tune your AI strategies based on performance data and user feedback.

The success stories from healthcare, marketing, education, and finance prove that generative AI is more than just a trend—it's a transformative tool that drives real-world results. Whether you're improving diagnostics in healthcare, crafting personalized marketing campaigns, offering tailored learning experiences in education, or optimizing investment strategies in finance, generative AI can propel your business to new heights. Take inspiration from these case studies and start exploring how you can harness the power of AI in your industry. The future is here, and with it comes boundless opportunities for growth, innovation, and success.

Chapter 5: Future-Proofing Your Skillset with Generative AI

The sky was painted in hues of orange and gold as Clara walked into the community center, her heart pounding with anticipation. Tonight, she was attending a workshop titled "Generative AI: The Key to Staying Relevant." Clara had always been ahead of the curve in her career, but as technology advanced at breakneck speed, she felt the weight of uncertainty.

The room was abuzz with energy. Professionals from diverse industries gathered, each grappling with the same question: How do we future-proof ourselves in a world reshaped by AI? At the front stood Samir, the charismatic instructor, who exuded confidence and warmth.

Samir began with a story. "Two years ago, I was at a crossroads. As a graphic designer, I watched AI tools churn out stunning visuals in seconds. Fear consumed me. But instead of resisting, I chose to collaborate with AI. Today, I'm not just a designer; I'm an AI-powered visual storyteller. Let me show you how you can find your path, too."

Embracing the AI Mindset

Samir's first lesson was about mindset. "Generative AI isn't here to replace you; it's here to amplify you," he said. He shared the story of Marcus, a chef who had been skeptical of AI in his kitchen. Marcus feared losing his creative touch, but after experimenting with an AI recipe generator, he discovered new flavor combinations he'd never considered. "The key was Marcus' willingness to explore," Samir explained. "Your mindset will determine whether AI becomes your ally or your adversary."

Clara found herself nodding. Her own hesitation stemmed from fear, not opportunity. She resolved to see AI as a partner in her journey.

Building Your AI Toolkit

The workshop transitioned to practical applications. Samir introduced the group to three key tools:

1. Text Generators: Platforms like ChatGPT and Jasper AI.
   2. Image Creators: Tools such as DALL-E and MidJourney.
   3. Data Analyzers: Applications like Tableau powered by AI algorithms.

"Imagine you're an architect," Samir said, turning to the crowd. "You're designing a sustainable building. By using generative AI, you can analyze thousands of design variations, select the most efficient, and incorporate creative elements unique to your vision."

He recounted the journey of Aisha, an urban planner who used AI to reimagine cityscapes. Aisha's project, which blended human intuition with AI analysis, became a model for urban development worldwide.

The room buzzed with excitement as participants envisioned how these tools could transform their fields.

Stories of Transformation

Samir shared another story, this time about Raj, a financial analyst. Raj had once dreaded monthly reporting, a tedious process prone to errors. After learning about AI-powered financial tools, Raj automated repetitive tasks and focused on providing insights. This not only elevated his role but made him an indispensable asset to his firm.

"What did Raj do differently?" Samir asked. He answered his own question: "He adapted. And he didn't stop there; he sought ways to integrate AI across his organization, becoming a change leader."

Clara's First Step

During a breakout session, Clara joined a group exercise to brainstorm ways AI could enhance their work. She met Luis, a middle-school teacher who had started using AI to craft personalized learning plans. "Generative AI analyzes my students' progress and creates tailored exercises," Luis explained. "It's like having a co-teacher who never sleeps."

Inspired, Clara imagined how AI could transform her role as a marketing strategist. What if she used AI to predict trends and design campaigns with precision? The possibilities felt endless.

Overcoming Challenges

Samir addressed the elephant in the room: challenges. "AI isn't perfect. It's only as good as the data you feed it," he cautioned. He narrated the experience of Elena, a journalist who had initially trusted AI to generate news articles. However, the AI inadvertently propagated biased narratives because its training data was flawed. Elena learned to pair AI outputs with her editorial judgment, striking a balance between efficiency and integrity.

This story resonated deeply with Clara. As she scribbled notes, she realized the importance of staying vigilant and ethical in her AI journey.

The Roadmap to Mastery

As the workshop neared its end, Samir presented a roadmap:

1. Learn: Identify industry-relevant AI tools and take courses to understand their potential.
2. Experiment: Start small. Use AI to tackle low-risk tasks and gradually integrate it into complex projects.
3. Collaborate: Join communities where professionals share AI success stories and challenges.
4. Innovate: Use AI to think beyond the obvious, creating solutions that didn't exist before.

He encouraged the group to embrace continuous learning. "The future isn't about knowing it all; it's about knowing how to adapt when everything changes."

Clara's Transformation

Months later, Clara stood before her own team, presenting a campaign that had taken her agency by storm. Using generative AI, Clara had identified untapped audiences and created content that resonated deeply. The results were staggering: a 40% increase in engagement and a renewed confidence in her leadership.

Clara's story became a beacon for others. She hosted AI workshops at her firm, fostering a culture of innovation and adaptability. Her journey wasn't just about mastering AI; it was about future-proofing her skillset and helping others do the same.

Writing Your Own Story

As you close this chapter, ask yourself: What's your story? Like Clara, Marcus, and Raj, you stand at the precipice of transformation. Generative AI isn't just a tool; it's a bridge to your future.

The next move is yours. Will you cross it?

Adapting to Evolving Technologies and Staying Ahead in a Rapidly Changing Landscape

In the contemporary world, characterized by relentless technological evolution, the capacity to adapt and remain ahead is more than a professional asset—it is a necessity. Organizations and individuals alike face the dual challenge of leveraging emerging technologies while navigating the disruptions they bring. This chapter explores strategic frameworks, real-world case studies, and actionable recommendations to equip professionals with the tools to thrive amidst rapid technological shifts.

Understanding the Pace of Change

Technological advancement is exponential. Gordon Moore's prediction, popularly known as Moore's Law, highlighted the doubling of computing power approximately every two years. While initially applied to semiconductors, this concept encapsulates the broader trajectory of technological development. This exponential growth has profound implications for businesses, as innovations such as generative AI, blockchain, and quantum computing reshape industries at an unprecedented pace.

Strategic Imperatives for Adapting to Change

1. Continuous Learning and Skill Development

The half-life of skills—the time during which skills remain relevant—is shrinking. Research by the World Economic Forum indicates that by 2027, over 40% of core skills for most jobs will have changed. Professionals must adopt a mindset of lifelong learning. Leading organizations such as IBM and Google have embraced upskilling programs, offering employees access to courses in artificial intelligence, data analytics, and cloud computing.

Case Study: The Reskilling Revolution at AT&T

Faced with rapid technological changes in telecommunications, AT&T launched its "Future Ready" initiative. The program identified critical skill gaps and offered employees financial incentives to pursue courses in areas like cybersecurity and data science. The result? Over 50% of employees engaged in reskilling efforts, enabling the company to maintain its competitive edge in an industry undergoing seismic shifts.

2. Leveraging Generative AI for Competitive Advantage

Generative AI exemplifies the transformative potential of emerging technologies. Tools like ChatGPT, DALL-E, and Codex are not merely augmenting workflows but fundamentally altering them. Companies adopting generative AI early gain significant advantages in efficiency, creativity, and innovation.

Case Study: Marketing Reinvented with Generative AI

A global consumer goods company integrated generative AI into its marketing department to automate the creation of ad copy and visual assets. By analyzing consumer behavior and trends, AI-generated campaigns achieved a 30% higher engagement rate compared to traditional methods. The strategic deployment of generative AI reduced time-to-market for campaigns by 40%, underscoring its potential to redefine marketing paradigms.

3. Building Agile Organizational Structures

Agility is the cornerstone of resilience in a rapidly changing landscape. Agile organizations prioritize cross-functional collaboration, iterative decision-making, and a willingness to pivot strategies in response to new information.

Case Study: Spotify's Agile Model

Spotify's "tribes" and "squads" structure exemplifies organizational agility. Teams operate autonomously within a cohesive framework, fostering innovation while maintaining alignment with broader company goals. This approach enabled Spotify to adapt swiftly to changes in user preferences and technological advancements, solidifying its position as a leader in the streaming industry.

4. Embracing Ecosystem Collaboration

No organization operates in isolation. Collaborative ecosystems—partnerships between startups, academia, and industry leaders—drive innovation by pooling resources and expertise. Platforms like MIT's Media Lab exemplify the power of collaborative innovation.

Case Study: OpenAI and Microsoft's Strategic Partnership

The collaboration between OpenAI and Microsoft illustrates the potential of ecosystem partnerships. By integrating OpenAI's generative AI capabilities into Microsoft's Azure platform, the partnership democratized access to cutting-edge AI tools, enabling businesses worldwide to innovate and scale rapidly.

Navigating Challenges in Technological Adoption

While the opportunities presented by emerging technologies are immense, they come with significant challenges:

1. Ethical Considerations

The deployment of technologies like AI must be guided by ethical principles. Issues such as data privacy, algorithmic bias, and the displacement of jobs necessitate robust governance frameworks.

Recommendation: Establish cross-disciplinary ethics boards to evaluate and mitigate potential risks associated with technology adoption.

2. Overcoming Resistance to Change

Resistance to change is a natural human response. Organizations must prioritize change management strategies, including clear communication, stakeholder involvement, and the demonstration of tangible benefits.

Recommendation: Employ frameworks like Kotter's 8-Step Change Model to systematically address resistance and foster buy-in.

3. Balancing Innovation with Security

The adoption of new technologies increases exposure to cybersecurity threats. As businesses integrate AI, IoT, and other advanced systems, they must simultaneously enhance their cybersecurity measures.

Case Study: Securing IoT in Smart Cities

A leading smart city initiative faced significant cyber threats due to its extensive IoT network. By implementing AI-driven cybersecurity solutions, the city identified and neutralized threats in real-time, ensuring the integrity of its critical infrastructure.

Recommendations for Staying Ahead

1. Adopt a Forward-Thinking Mindset

Strategic foresight involves anticipating future trends and preparing for multiple scenarios. Tools like scenario planning and trend analysis are invaluable for organizations aiming to stay ahead.

Actionable Tip: Encourage leaders to engage with foresight methodologies and participate in industry think tanks to identify emerging trends.

2. Invest in Emerging Technologies

Early adoption of technologies like quantum computing, blockchain, and AI can provide a competitive edge. However, investments must be strategic and aligned with long-term business goals.

Actionable Tip: Conduct pilot projects to evaluate the feasibility and ROI of adopting new technologies.

3. Foster a Culture of Experimentation

Organizations that prioritize experimentation and accept failure as a learning process are better positioned to innovate.

Actionable Tip: Allocate resources for R&D initiatives and establish innovation hubs within the organization.

Adapting to evolving technologies and staying ahead requires a multifaceted approach that blends continuous learning, strategic foresight, and a willingness to embrace change. By analyzing case studies, adopting proven frameworks, and fostering a culture of agility and collaboration, professionals and organizations can not only navigate but thrive in a rapidly changing landscape. The future belongs to those who are prepared to adapt today.

Section	Key Insights	Examples/Case Studies
Understanding the Pace of Change	Technological evolution is exponential, impacting industries like AI, blockchain, and quantum computing.	Moore's Law illustrates rapid advancements in computing power.
Continuous Learning	The half-life of skills is shrinking; upskilling is critical to remain competitive.	AT&T's "Future Ready" initiative helped employees reskill in data science and cybersecurity.
Generative AI Usage	Early adopters gain efficiency and creativity.	A consumer goods company improved marketing engagement by 30% using generative AI.
Agile Structures	Agility fosters resilience; cross-functional teams adapt faster.	Spotify's "tribes" and "squads" enable innovation and alignment.
Ecosystem Collaboration	Partnerships boost innovation through shared expertise and resources.	OpenAI and Microsoft's collaboration democratized AI tools via Azure.
Ethical Considerations	Technology use must align with ethical governance to mitigate risks like data bias.	Organizations should establish ethics boards to oversee AI implementation.
Resistance to Change	Change management frameworks ease adoption and increase buy-in.	Kotter's 8-Step Model offers a systematic approach to overcoming resistance.
Cybersecurity in New Tech	Innovation increases exposure to cyber threats, requiring robust security strategies.	Smart cities using AI-driven solutions neutralized IoT threats in real time.
Future-Oriented Thinking	Strategic foresight enables preparation for trends and disruptions.	Scenario planning helps leaders anticipate shifts in technology and market dynamics.
Investment in Emerging Tech	Early technology adoption aligns with long-term strategic goals.	Pilot projects assess quantum computing and blockchain's ROI.
Culture of Experimentation	Encouraging experimentation and embracing failure drives innovation.	Organizations establishing R&D hubs improve their adaptability and creativity.

This statistical summary encapsulates key findings, actionable insights, and illustrative examples from the document, streamlining the essential content for strategic application.

Appendices for Master Generative AI in Minutes: Advanced Strategies, Practical Solutions, and Case Studies for Busy Professionals

Appendix A: Essential Tools and Resources

Navigating the vast ecosystem of generative AI tools and resources can be daunting. This appendix provides a curated selection of essential tools, platforms, and guides tailored for busy professionals aiming to accelerate their generative AI journey. Each entry is selected based on its practicality, efficiency, and proven track record in delivering results.

1. Generative AI Platforms

OpenAI's GPT-4
   - Overview: A state-of-the-art language model capable of generating human-like text, coding, summarization, and creative writing.
   - Use Cases: Content creation, customer service automation, and personalized learning experiences.
   - Key Features: Advanced contextual understanding and integration with API services.
   - Website: [OpenAI](https://openai.com)

Google Bard
   - Overview: A versatile tool for generating text and conducting real-time queries using the latest advancements in AI.
   - Use Cases: Ideation, competitive analysis, and real-time query handling.
   - Key Features: Easy integration with Google's ecosystem, including Docs and Sheets.
   - Website: [Google Bard](https://bard.google.com)

DALL-E 3

- Overview: An image-generation platform by OpenAI that transforms text prompts into detailed visuals.
- Use Cases: Marketing campaigns, product design, and visual storytelling.
- Key Features: Fine-tuned control over style, color, and composition.
- Website: [DALL-E](https://openai.com/dall-e)

2. Development and Experimentation Tools

Hugging Face

- Overview: A hub for pre-trained models and datasets in natural language processing (NLP), computer vision, and more.
- Use Cases: Quick experimentation with models and fine-tuning custom solutions.
- Key Features: Easy integration with Python libraries and APIs.
- Website: [Hugging Face](https://huggingface.co)

Runway ML

- Overview: A user-friendly platform for video editing and content creation using AI.
- Use Cases: Enhancing video content, generating animations, and applying special effects.
- Key Features: Intuitive drag-and-drop interface with AI-powered editing tools.
- Website: [Runway ML](https://runwayml.com)

3. Data Management and Annotation Tools

Label Studio

- Overview: An open-source tool for data labeling and annotation.
- Use Cases: Preparing datasets for training AI models.
- Key Features: Supports multiple formats and seamless collaboration.
- Website: [Label Studio](https://labelstudio.io)

Databricks
- Overview: A collaborative data platform for building AI solutions at scale.
- Use Cases: Managing large datasets, running machine learning workflows, and collaborative analysis.
- Key Features: Robust integration with cloud storage and visualization tools.
- Website: [Databricks](https://databricks.com)

4. Learning and Skill-Building Resources

Coursera's AI for Everyone
- Overview: A beginner-friendly course by Andrew Ng.
- Use Cases: Understanding foundational concepts in AI and machine learning.
- Key Features: Real-world examples and industry applications.
- Website: [Coursera](https://www.coursera.org/learn/ai-for-everyone)

DeepLearning.AI
- Overview: Comprehensive programs for professionals to master AI concepts.
- Use Cases: Skill-building in neural networks, generative AI, and applied AI.
- Key Features: Expert-led courses with practical exercises.
- Website: [DeepLearning.AI](https://www.deeplearning.ai)

5. Productivity and Workflow Tools

Notion AI
- Overview: An AI-powered extension for productivity within the Notion workspace.
- Use Cases: Automating note-taking, summarizing meeting discussions, and generating action items.
- Key Features: Seamless integration with Notion's organization tools.
- Website: [Notion](https://www.notion.so)

Zapier
- Overview: A platform for automating repetitive tasks by connecting apps and workflows.
- Use Cases: Streamlining data transfers between generative AI tools and existing systems.
- Key Features: Extensive library of app integrations.
- Website: [Zapier](https://zapier.com)

6. Community and Collaboration Resources

Kaggle
- Overview: A community for data scientists to share projects, datasets, and solutions.
- Use Cases: Participating in AI competitions and accessing free educational resources.
- Key Features: Interactive notebooks and a collaborative environment.
- Website: [Kaggle](https://www.kaggle.com)

Slack AI Communities
- Overview: Niche communities for professionals in AI to exchange ideas and collaborate.
- Use Cases: Networking, troubleshooting, and staying updated on trends.
- Key Features: Real-time collaboration with industry experts.
- Website: [Slack](https://slack.com)

Appendix B: Common Challenges and Quick Fixes

Generative AI adoption can be fraught with challenges, especially for busy professionals. This appendix addresses common issues and offers practical solutions to streamline your AI journey.

1. Prompt Engineering Challenges

Issue: Generating irrelevant or suboptimal outputs.
- Quick Fix: Refine your prompts by being specific about the desired output. Use clear instructions, examples, and constraints to guide the model.

- Example: Instead of "Generate a marketing plan," specify "Generate a social media marketing plan for a tech startup targeting Gen Z."
- Pro Tip: Experiment with iterative prompting to fine-tune results.

Issue: Understanding the model's capabilities and limitations.
- Quick Fix: Refer to the official documentation of the tool (e.g., OpenAI's GPT-4 documentation) to learn about its strengths and weaknesses.

2. Data Privacy and Security

Issue: Concerns over sharing sensitive data with AI platforms.
- Quick Fix: Use tools that guarantee end-to-end encryption and on-premise deployment. Avoid sharing proprietary data in publicly hosted models.
- Example Tools: Run your models locally using platforms like Hugging Face or private instances of GPT models.

3. Cost Management

Issue: Unexpectedly high expenses for API usage.
- Quick Fix: Set usage caps and monitor API consumption through dashboards provided by the platform. Use cost-effective alternatives like open-source models for non-critical tasks.
- Pro Tip: Optimize token usage by crafting concise prompts and responses.

4. Integration Issues

Issue: Difficulty integrating AI tools with existing workflows.
- Quick Fix: Leverage middleware platforms like Zapier to connect disparate systems. Alternatively, use APIs provided by the AI tool for custom integrations.

Issue: Lack of technical expertise to implement AI solutions.
- Quick Fix: Utilize low-code/no-code platforms such as Runway ML or explore pre-configured tools.
- Pro Tip: Engage with freelancers or consultants for initial setups.

5. Ethical and Bias Concerns

Issue: AI generating biased or inappropriate content.
 - Quick Fix: Pre-test prompts in a controlled environment and use filters or moderation layers. Implement ethical AI guidelines in your organization.
 - Example: Incorporate feedback loops to identify and address bias in generated outputs.

6. Keeping Up with Rapid Advancements

Issue: Struggling to stay updated on the latest tools and trends.
 - Quick Fix: Subscribe to newsletters, join AI-focused forums, and attend webinars hosted by industry leaders. Leverage resources like AI-specific LinkedIn groups.

7. Model Performance Limitations

Issue: Slow response times or degraded performance during high-demand periods.
 - Quick Fix: Opt for higher-tier service plans with priority access or deploy models on private infrastructure.

Issue: Limited creativity or rigidity in responses.
 - Quick Fix: Use creative writing prompts to push the model beyond standard patterns. Enable advanced features like fine-tuning where available.

8. Troubleshooting Technical Errors

Issue: Error codes or system crashes during operation.
 - Quick Fix: Refer to the troubleshooting section of the platform's documentation. Common solutions include clearing cache, updating software, or restarting sessions.
 - Pro Tip: Maintain logs to track recurring issues and streamline support requests.

Appendix C: Glossary of Generative AI Terms

Understanding the specialized language of generative AI is essential for navigating this complex field. Below is a glossary of key terms, simplified for quick reference by busy professionals:

A

- **AI Ethics**: The study and practice of moral implications and responsibilities in the development and deployment of artificial intelligence systems.
- **API (Application Programming Interface)**: A set of rules that allows different software applications to communicate with each other. APIs are often used to integrate AI models into existing workflows.
- **Artificial Neural Network (ANN)**: A computational model inspired by the human brain, consisting of layers of interconnected nodes (neurons) that process data.

B

- **Bias (in AI)**: A systematic error in AI models caused by imbalanced or unrepresentative training data, leading to unfair or inaccurate results.
- **Backpropagation**: A learning algorithm used in training neural networks by adjusting weights based on the error rate of previous predictions.

C

- **Contextual Understanding**: The ability of AI to interpret text or data within the framework of its surrounding information, improving relevance and accuracy.
- **Corpus**: A large collection of texts or datasets used to train natural language processing models.

D

- **Deep Learning**: A subset of machine learning focused on algorithms inspired by the structure and function of the brain's neural networks.
- **Diffusion Models**: A type of generative model used to create high-quality images, audio, or text by iteratively improving random noise into meaningful content.

F

- **Fine-Tuning**: The process of training a pre-trained AI model on a specific dataset to improve its performance on a particular task.
- **Few-Shot Learning**: A training paradigm where the model learns to perform tasks with very few examples.

G
- **GAN (Generative Adversarial Network)**: A generative AI framework involving two networks, a generator and a discriminator, that work in opposition to create realistic outputs.
- **Generative AI**: Artificial intelligence systems capable of creating new content, such as text, images, or music, based on input data.

L
- **Language Model**: A machine learning model designed to understand and generate human-like language.
- **Latent Space**: A representation of compressed data that generative models use to create outputs.

P
- **Prompt Engineering**: The practice of designing input queries to guide AI models toward generating desired outputs.
- **Pre-trained Model**: A model that has been trained on a large dataset and can be fine-tuned for specific tasks.

T
- **Tokenization**: The process of breaking text into smaller units, such as words or subwords, for input into a model.
- **Transformer**: A neural network architecture used in many state-of-the-art language models, such as GPT-4.

Z
- **Zero-Shot Learning**: The ability of an AI model to perform a task without having been explicitly trained on examples of that task.

Appendix D: Ethical Considerations and Best Practices

The integration of generative AI into professional settings necessitates a commitment to ethical practices to avoid unintended consequences and maintain trust.

1. Core Ethical Principles

Transparency
- Clearly disclose the use of AI in generated content, especially in customer-facing applications.
- Example: Label AI-generated emails or advertisements to maintain credibility.

Fairness
- Mitigate biases in AI outputs by using diverse datasets and implementing fairness audits.
- Case Study: A healthcare provider reduced disparities in AI predictions by retraining models on a balanced dataset.

Accountability
- Assign responsibility for AI decisions to human supervisors. Ensure an audit trail for all AI-driven processes.
- Recommendation: Develop an internal ethics committee to oversee AI deployments.

2. Privacy and Data Security

Principle: Protect user and organizational data during AI interactions.
- **Best Practice**: Use anonymized datasets and encrypted communication channels.
- **Example**: A financial institution deployed on-premise AI models to ensure compliance with data protection laws.

Principle: Minimize data collection to reduce risk.
- **Best Practice**: Adopt "data minimization" strategies by only gathering what is essential for AI performance.

3. Avoiding Misuse

Generative AI can inadvertently enable unethical practices, such as misinformation or deepfake creation.

Guideline: Restrict access to high-risk capabilities.
- **Example**: Companies limit the resolution of AI-generated images to prevent misuse in counterfeiting.

Guideline: Implement robust moderation tools.
- **Example**: Use AI-powered filters to detect and block inappropriate content in real time.

4. Promoting Inclusivity

Ensure generative AI outputs reflect a broad spectrum of perspectives.

Guideline: Train models on diverse datasets.

- **Example**: An educational AI platform incorporated multilingual datasets to support global users.

Guideline: Engage diverse stakeholders in model evaluation.
- **Case Study**: A tech firm reduced cultural biases by involving regional experts in testing AI outputs.

5. Best Practices for Responsible Use

Encourage Cross-Functional Collaboration
- Foster teamwork between technical experts, legal advisors, and business leaders to align AI initiatives with organizational values.

Invest in Continuous Training
- Provide employees with training on ethical AI usage and potential pitfalls.
- Recommendation: Include AI ethics as part of corporate onboarding programs.

Monitor and Adapt
- Regularly review AI implementations to adapt to new regulations and societal expectations.
- Example: A retailer revised its AI-driven pricing model to align with emerging consumer protection laws.

Conclusion

By adhering to these ethical considerations and adopting best practices, professionals can harness generative AI responsibly, maximizing its potential while safeguarding against risks.

END

www.ingramcontent.com/pod-product-compliance
Lightning Source LLC
Chambersburg PA
CBHW071110240526
45469CB00006BD/2423